EARTH HOUSE

Matthew Hollis is the author of *Ground Water* (Bloodaxe Books), shortlisted for the Guardian First Book Award and the Whitbread Award for Poetry in 2004. *Now All Roads Lead to France: the Last Years of Edward Thomas* (Faber & Faber) won the Costa Biography Award and was *Sunday Times* Biography of the Year, 2011. Small-press pamphlets include *Stones* (Incline Press), 2016, and *Leaves* (Hazel Press), shortlisted for the Michael Marks Award, 2021. *The Waste Land: A Biography of a Poem* (Faber & Faber) was a Book of the Year in the *Financial Times*, *New Statesman* and *Sunday Times*, 2022. *Earth House* (Bloodaxe Books) was longlisted for the Laurel Prize for Poetry 2023. It was a Book of the Year and Summer Reading Choice in the *Tablet*, Poetry Book of the Month on BBC Radio 4 Extra and a featured poem in the *Guardian*, *Telegraph*, *Traveller* magazine and *Yorkshire Times*.

'It's taken Matthew Hollis 19 years to produce a successor to his debut
collection, *Ground Water*, but *Earth House* was worth the wait.
Well-nigh elemental in their evocation of time and landscape,
the poems . . . are consummate exercises in psychogeography,
where, however ancient the terrain, the people lead the dance.'
D.J. TAYLOR, *Tablet*, Summer Reading

A sweeping meditation on time, history, and our place in the natural world.'
MAGGIE WANG, *Poetry Book Society Bulletin*

'Enchanting . . . what good poems.'
RONALD BLYTHE, author of *Akenfield*

'His quietly distinguished, wise and elegant poems, on the earth
and our fluid, unsettled place in it, are always a pleasure
to spend time with . . . The impact is quietly devastating.'
NICOLA HEALEY, *London Magazine*

'Attuned to the interconnections between landscape, language and ecology, Matthew Hollis' *Earth House* is an astounding and deeply immersive collection that moves from elegiac loss to the birth of new life. Musical, layered and reflective, the poems magnify the environmental tremors we so often wreak in our wake, all the while suggesting the quiet possibility of another, more attentive way of being in the world, premised before anything on astonishment.'
NIKOLAI DUFFY, *Tablet*, Books of the Year

'Myth and language keep the past ever-present for Hollis: his work is steeped in allusions to Anglo Saxon, Celtic and Norse myth, and richly textured with regional discourse, anchoring language both to history and place...a stunning collection.'
PAUL McDONALD, *London Grip*

'Hollis writes with an unsentimental love of the natural world, in poems where landscapes he knows well are charged with a personal significance that's often only hinted at.'
TRISTRAM FANE SAUNDERS, *Telegraph*, Poem of the Week

'This is poetry as music...that leaves the reader caught between savouring what the poet has just done and hungering for the next line. If it were a song on Spotify you'd have it on repeat.'
CARL TOMLINSON, *Friday Poem*

Praise for STONES *and* LEAVES

'A song of seasonal degeneration and rejuvenation...
an incantatory rhythm that quietly but insistently interrogates the ecological future of the planet and laments the carelessness with which it is treated.'
DFIZA BENSON, *Poetry Review*

'Magnificent.'
PAUL FARLEY, *Echo Chamber*, BBC Radio 4

Earth House

MATTHEW HOLLIS

BLOODAXE BOOKS

ISBN: 978 1 78037 622 6

First published 2023 by
Bloodaxe Books Ltd
Eastburn
South Park
Hexham
Northumberland NE46 1BS
This paperback first published in 2024

www.bloodaxebooks.com
For further information about Bloodaxe titles
please visit our website and join our mailing list
or write to the above address for a catalogue

Supported using public funding by
ARTS COUNCIL
ENGLAND

Cover artist: Jonathan Gibbs
Cover design: Eleanor Crow
Text design: Small.Fish

Printed in Great Britain by Bell & Bain Limited, Glasgow, Scotland,
on acid-free paper sourced from mills with FSC chain of custody certification

for James & Rose

Contents

I

II

III

IV

EARTH HOUSE

Causeway

Beneath the rain⁄shadow and washed farmhouses,
in the service of the old shore,

we waited for the rising of the road,
the south lane laden in sand,

the north in residue and wrack;
the tide drawing off the asphalt

leaving our tyres little to disperse;
still, the water under wheel was forceful –

cleft between the chassis and the sea –
that clean division that the heart rages for.

But halfway out the destination ceases to be the prize,
and what matters is the sudden breadth of vision:

to the north, a hovering headland,
to the south, a shoal of light –

the sea off⁄guarded, but hunting:
our licence brief, unlikely to be renewed.

Between mainland and island, in neither sway,
a nodding of the needle as the compass takes its weigh.

The Sea Stick

The low tide brings her in,
scouring the surf-line
for dogweed and jellies,
stones coughed from the sea.

What interests her more
is the take of wood
that she gathers for the fire.
She knows how things burn,

beginning with the kindling:
birch bark and fir cones,
dust from the wood wasps,
dried grasses, wisp cotton, a feather.

Then the fragments of spark-wood:
willow and cedar, an arrow
of spruce, to have
the flame go higher.

What interests her most
is the hardwood: some oak
or beech to split and stack,
to bear the weight of winter.

But this tide brings something strange:
straightened wood, an arm in length.
It is not much, but in her mind
it might be

a cane or staff or walking stick,
a tottering strut to take the strain,
a shepherd's crook, a stake, a spear,
a plinth to prop the coal-shed door,

a chair back or a table leg,
the foot to foot a lovers' bed,
a linen pole, a curtain rail,
a prank pushed through a bicycle wheel,

a scullery brush, a mop handle,
the haft that held the malt shovel,
a flag mast, fence post, drover's prod,
a hobby horse, a child's crib,

a witch's broom; and most of all
a toy flute, yet to be bored,
that she puts to her lips and blows upon –
as if raising a tune from the old life.

Beck

The brim that broke the river came on land.
Its skirts were vast from so much rain and made
the grass beneath it dance, wild hair of the drowned.
We trailed it to the road, where a cattle grid
gulped it down and where a hedgehog whirled
in its mitten of thorns. Back then, we sought
such life, and found a plank and edged it in;
but the urchin would not climb to his escape.

By morning the grid had emptied, the wood
snapped clean in two. You supposed a fox
or brock had dug the creature out.
I wanted to believe he'd made it home.
But faith in faith is not enough.
We go on love alone.

4

Wastwater

Then, when you have remembered to forget,
I will trouble you again to follow me
across three shires and a river's source
and over the steepest pass; – late,
in a year like this, when the weather
is hard at the hem of the car,
and you steady the wheel, reminded of your place,
and look down on the scarp with its paper-
clip turns, the tyres quarrying for grip.
Hard to make sense of, but you descend
gladdened and breathless, rushed with life,
yet partly cheated, half wanting to be blown
to the corners of beyond; – late,
on a day like this, at the waters
of the deepest lake, when the clouds are filthy
and wind rips down the scree, and you turn to face,
seeking yourself in the chamber of this,
when something like your own life
comes thundering over the water towards you.

A White Hart at Sykeside

Some days I have found myself,
in February or early March,
watching the plum tree bruised with blossom,
new light waking from the carpet

the peat-brown oil
we used to glue you to your skin,
your turf-cut body a tannery then,
thinned where the bog first entered in.

Days in doorways dead of breeze
the scent dissolves; but spring–summer mornings,
when warm air works its way beneath the sills,
your transparency rises, and goes about the halls.

Once, I saw or almost saw you.
A quarter to the midnight that you died.
Half-cut, coming back from the village,
I called out for you then, in the unshamed way

of the drowning and the drunk,
when from the tarn, behind the house,
a white hart came. Whether it was moonlight
or wishfulness that made it flare

I can't now know, but the air about it
seemed to blaze unnaturally.
All skid and clatter on the cold stone,
it bounded the coping of the garden wall

into the alley six feet below,
wilding at its sudden walling on three sides:
one end stoppered by an old coal hut;
above, a slot of unlidded light;

ahead, the entrance at which I stood,
which now it took for all its worth.
I dove – as much for the surety of stone
as preservation. For whichever it was –

the real caller, crossed briefly into breath,
or some mere trickery – I hardly minded,
for its heat and the taut flank that clipped me
were true enough. I saw it slipshod

on the cobbles, cornering rough,
its centrifuge breaking forth,
those hard hoofs sparking for foothold,
igniting the momentary, the ungraspable earth.

All there ever is

I climbed to find myself alone
as sun gave into rain and then to hail,
and something unfamiliar urged me
from the safety of Stone Arthur
for the unknown ridge of Heron Pike.
Of all my coming deaths I never thought
I'd run to them. But there the wind
threw in so hard it made my legs its own
and swept me all at sprint towards the edge.
I cast down inches from the drop –
a bone and bloodied grip against extinction.
What rose to drag itself to ground
was no grown man facing out his fear,
but a child who sensed its dream of adulthood
had gone. And something more like prayer:
something answered in the life we lead,
a common fire, a heat to come home for,
and not to find it bare – this wind and rock
between us, that's all there ever is.

Call

She, the geese lifting off the lake.
He, a feather, a broken egg.
She, the blaw of the knuckled crag.
He, the battering bracken.
She, the tarn, the tarn's sore lip.
He, a glass and a running tap.
She, the gill, the scree, the tor.
She, the wheat fire, crack of thorns.
She, the punch of wind in the lungs,
A chute or sail or alike blown open.
He, indoors, keeping it even.
She to the shore with a bucket of foam.
He to the hills with a fist of stones.

Stones

I

The sea is a land in waiting.
Each morning, each evening
it turns out its pockets for the strandline:
a starfish plaything, an unwrapped cuttle,
some days a mermaid's purse.
These were the jewels when the jewels were living.
And when there were no jewels there were stones,
pebbles, the pennies of the sea.
Whether we went together or alone
it was these that we scooped and carried home
to stack in a jar by the door.
Always we gathered too many,
and those we dropped behind us became girls and boys,
those lain in the wash became sea again,
their bones became water, their muscles foam,
the sea shall call her children home.
That is the deal, that much is known:
from water into the air we are thrown,
and what we make of it from there
is what makes us our own.
The dunes are stocked with shoes and socks,
and laughter rings beyond the rocks.
The stones we drop grow into men and women.
Those that renege on the shore become sea again.
The land is a sea in waiting.

II

There will be hours, hours to come,
hours when it seems to either one
the other is incapable
of drawing breath into the lungs,
when death has woken in the bone
of what was thought invincible.

The difference then will not be
in the faculty to love but to let go:
some are holders, fighters, keepers⁄on;
others repair for the measurement of ground.

The stronger still turn back to life.

I am living you are living
he she they are living –

Either we had our time or we'll have
our time or our time is now –

but time is not what we have been denied
and shall be ample when we come to comb
the way the chances bound and broke.
My father took a county train to Addenbrookes,
and not remembering his doctor's name,
and not liking to ask, turned unseen for home again.
Was that his chance? With the folding of the papers,
will we have said that we took hold of ours?

The carter and the cart untie.
The furnace from the firefly.

III

An old brown flour-barrel in the yard
reads OUR from the angle of the road.
There's no miller now to keep it in
and so its use has turned to making mulch
to feed the apple roots that pin the upper field.
A pair of grindstones stand here too:
one, a make-do platform, overlooks a dale,
the other marks an entrance to a moor.
Use may change but use itself goes on.

You said once that any life beyond this one
would be component, atomic, ourselves
broken down and remade into other things:
the soil, the forest, the beetles and the seas,
even the sedimentary stones.
Perhaps nothing but the body truly dies,
and the past becomes a room within the present
that we learn to live around, locked or ajar
depending on the kind of keeper that we are.

At every stroke of every hour we change;
we change, and therein lies the curse and cure.
Move on, move on, the tattlers say,
but we do not move on: we subdue
the riot, and learn to man the doors
between the present and the past.
Foolish to think it was ever about forgiveness:
which one of us confers such higher ground?

IV

As the hill climbs so it tails,
in plain view or an unseen vale,
it must descend to keep the living level.
I don't know why it comes as a surprise:
the universe is neither cruel nor kind.
More and more the days pour out the same.
A basin slowly fills and drains,
the dustmen dally in the lane,
and Thursdays turn to Fridays
as the banks take back their bets,
and working minds dissolve
into ever onward space.
Sand, soda-ash and lime.
The universe is neither cruel nor kind.

Beneath the weeping beech at Kew
I met a man who said he knew
each tree was talking to the next,
he simply couldn't prove it, yet.

The houses are in ruins,
but a ruin is just a home for things
that are not needed now.
And now our need must reach beyond
the hunger of the present, to find a place
where harm was done and know it done
to the past performers of ourselves.
A hallway lined with infant shoes.
Raining in rooms that once had roofs.

V

Descending from the tarn that day,
a hand in yours, the other raised for balance,
I felt sure that we knew happiness,
and reached into the waters of the gill
for something to give you,
and lifted from the bed a small red stone.
Straightening, I turned to see you
moving to me with a same red stone,
exchanged, then, without a word.

I kept those stones in a two⁄stone stack
neatly on the mantel⁄ledge
and could not move to throw them out
when every other trace had gone.

I had driven no more than a mile
before I knew I could carry them no further,
and turned back for the gill and held them under
until I could not feel my hand at all,
to sit forever in the same water,
or for as long as it takes for the currents
to pull them apart.

VI

Now that there is shade across the lawn,
and a settlement of birdsong,
and between the alleyways and houses
a telephone rings and someone answers,
and someone else is mowing grass:
I feel the day get hazier.
Was that rose or rhododendron
at the bottom of the garden?
How can I keep the sense of this
when sight and sound have gone?

You may be asked
if you knew the cost when you began
would you continue. You may be asked
if you'd undo what's done.
To answer
is to enter into the endless corridor,
into the orchard where nothing grew;
the child who tips its drink into a lake
and tries in vain to bail it back.

Part of each will carry in the other,
in the ether and the oak,
in bone or blood or smoke.

It may not be the telling that we chose,
but it is our own, for lesser or better:
recalling that once it was solely for better.

What passes in the present is present in the past.
And there it lies upon the latch.
Our hands tremble on the morning match.

The stones have grown into women and men.
Those that renege become sea again.

The land and the sea are in waiting.

The Long Snow

As the drift grew deeper he pressed on,
to where it cupped his ankle and his calf.
On, above his knee, around his waist,
until it held him fast. And there he stood,
unable to return or to advance.
And so he carried on inside his mind,
the ground untrod, a hood of cold,
through fields that meet no gateway or no road.

Lone

from the Anglo-Saxon

I make this song from a sad self,
my own journey. Many are the sorrows
since childhood, but no more than now,
this endless exile.

     Lord, my lord,
far over the seas, your people forsaken
since you went I know not where, and I woke
unhappy and alone; though I did as you asked –
walked friendless into hiding.

         But your kinsman
schemed of breaking our wedlock –
he whom I took for a friend
has put a lie between us.

       I followed
your bidding, went where you wanted,
where the friends were few, and found one
who mirrored me, a trusted one,
who beneath his care had a murderous mind.

 You made me a vow. You said
that nothing on this earth should divide us save dying.
And that has changed, as if never spoken.
Now I fear that you would take my name,
would harm me on the words of a false friend.

You sent me into a wooded grove
under an oak tree, a roof of roots,
an earth-hall held with longing.
Unlit valleys, a towering peak,
hamlets overcome with thorns —
here, your absence held me.

Some people on this earth wake close
to one another, are together at dawn,
but not us; I go apart, carrying for you,
a lifetime of days.
                    Always in youth
is a sadness that must wear itself within,
the same for freeman as outlaw.
                              Husband,
wherever this may find you — weary and waitsome,
in some hollow place or further shore,
you will remember, how it was
before the sorrow came.

No good love comes of longing.

II

Anglia

When the city exhausts you, when your marriage
is raw, and the young one cannot help himself
but drive you somewhere in,

                    pull back a while,
and take in mind the train ride into Anglia,
its northward draw across the muds at Manningtree,
where tide is tipping at the breach, the swans at gyre,
the sunlight slamming off the water

                           and into your eyes,
till you shield them for the longer view,
for what lies out on the river's rope,
the sea loosened and at call,
your breath hauling within you,
woken from the carriage into light.

Iken

Still there are moments when the wilding wakes,
to shake the withies in their heels of mud
below Long Reach, or Iken Cliff, where Botwulf
purged his demons, and laid his stone at Icenho.
Hard to hear it in sun and still water,
but in dawn or dusk⁄gloom, the wind in whurl,
that bellowing might be Grendel of
Grundisburgh, or whatever the creature
that slaughtered the masons at Yarn Hill,
and moved their stones in the night.

A Harnser for James

Gillying on Blakeney quay,
your young hands harrying the line

as another crab gives up its grip
for the safety of the estuary,

and your five-year face flares with frustration
at this world so slow to reward.

How far you are from patience still,
from coaxing more from less,

wound in ties and single threads
as yet too subtle for your engineering.

But even the harnser in his reed bed, there,
had once to learn to stalk and bait and spear –

And what's a harnser, anyway? you ask.
All the printed names you've yet to learn,

then the county words, worn at the ear,
passed in playgrounds and childhood towns:

The harnser is the heron.
And something in your worldhood fires, *What else?*

The mavish is the singing thrush,
the fulfer is the mistle thrush,

the miller, mothy at his lamp
was once a canker on the branch.

The crescent-tailed erriwiggle.
The jacob and the pollywiggle.

The dodman or the hodmedod.
The develin and the barley-bird.

The colony of pishamires.
The ranny in the field grass.

The guises of the hare we knew:
bandy, sally, sukey, sue.

The jasper jaunty at his fruit.
The hay-jack in his haysele suit.

The minifer, the merrymay.
The hoss, the hin, the bishybarnabee —

Cast down from your casting thread,
your fists punch in their pockets:

yet to work their catch, it's true,
but yet to humble any living creature.

Some days it seems enough to make it through
unharming and unharmed,

to keep the veil of gentleness from wearing out.
Other days will come within your calling,

practised and articulate and rhymed,
though now it feels like workfulness or forgery,

though now it feels hard-won: stay with me,
if you can, you will take up the line.

Winterton Ness

Not the stirrup of sea smoke you sometimes get,
nor a fogbank pale out of Frisia,
but a roke so thick and densely set
that leaving the car for the open dune
the sea itself was hidden –
only the brawl of it guiding one shoulder,
the other steered by the wind through the marram,
the sand white and frozen, these three–
four yards of vision.
      Downwind a dog bark,
upwind the *tup*
    tup of a boy playing keepy-up,
and the news of a newborn tapping
at our temples, our own parenthood untried;
the desire to lose ourselves so catered for
that we startled at the loom of the half-
drawn seals when it came,
and further on, more pencil than pen,
a sole pup sacked from a hardened sea.
It scared us, the peril and orphancy;
knowing a cub turned into the waves may drown.
But a dog's loose, and there're gulls to blind it,
and exposure and hunger, and sometimes it angers –
this furious indifference, this failure
to intervene.

Sometimes we barely do
much better: so frightened to make omission
that we make no impression at all.
Four times the pup hauled itself to sea
and was rebuffed. On the fifth,
I put my knee to the silt, prepared now
to carry it out, when it broke the surf
and slipped through a door in the ocean.
                                        How long

we stayed unsighted on the sand
I couldn't tell, but strand and the sketch
of dune secured us back. No dog, no bark,
just roar and edge, the wind at reel.
A lone car in a car park; a football
lodged between our bumper and our wheel.

I will lift up my eyes

She wonders where I am these days,
and if I've heard a word she's said.

But I watched the whimbrel in the wetlands,
an avocet shake its doubtful head,

and heard the cockles gossip
at the days-end of the tide.

Perhaps I climbed the ridge
and saw further than any Roman did,

and felt the wind that reached me there
unopposed and raw, the ringed hands

of two hundred Nordic miles and more.
Perhaps that's why, when I saw the turbines

turning out to sea, I thought of Mjölnir
whirling on its wrist of god,

or some equal engine of the uncurated earth,
and watched the rain drag its linen over Lincolnshire;

I wondered one day east if I'd see Ameland.
Inland, the talk's of summer homes half-filled.

But I heard, between the settlements,
the language shift by minutes and degrees,

where swinners turn to gillies
below the purslane and the thrift,

and felt the shingle⁄spit beneath my toes,
pick⁄pocket of volcanoes.

I had no hills to lift my eyes
so found an open theatre of the skies.

But dammit did I hear a word she said.
And don't I wonder where she is these days.

Where narrow water widens

Out in the mile, in the whale graves of wherries,
where the blunt hulls rot in their ribs
and the black frost grips like a warden's rings,
the winter marsh takes turns with the heart —
hammers it, then lays it out to starve.
There are safer grounds for man and wife:
in spring, when lapwings sing like firemen
firing up their siren, or summer,
as spiderlings kite on their gossamer;
but November, the silk lines heavy as hawser,
two tides press at a deadlock floe,
while a golden plover, that flustered butler,
runs its sculleries of ice. And nearing
the shore-fort we rout a field mouse
into the quarter of a harrier, who slips
from her shelf of air, and drops —
pairs a red sock inside out.
Sometimes our trouble is being there.
Better without us all of this life.

The Island

Some other day I will reach our only island.
Some day not today, when the ferry
won't take me into rain, and I've no child
to drown. That day, on a falling swell,
I will cross the Burn at Gun Hill, some day
not today. Not for me the Plover Marsh,
the Long Hills over Cockle Bight;
no brink beyond the ternery.
Some other day, I will reach Far Point,
where the winds cease up at the old wreck,
and the sea swings for all that is enemy,
like someone lost to a ball of bees.

Rooks

I

When the mark is lifted from your body,
the ghost chased from beneath your skin,
and we learn, as every living creature must,
to heal again,
              remember what it was
that brought us here, to a marsh
in midwinter, in a gathering dusk,
as roads root into shadow.
Night comes nearer each night;
so we rely on what we absorbed by light:
the gradient, the ground to foot, the hollow track –
whatever we know to be there – out
where sense would swear there is nothing
to harm us but our fear.
                 How reckless it seems
to let it come in and do nothing to prevent it –
not to reach for the car keys or phone,
not to be thinking for torchlight, home,
but laying down our upper hand
and facing into the whelm.
                  Remember, then,
what brought us here under lengthening dark,
climbing the lane to the inking oaks
as the birds begin to gather.

II

                  At first
there is barely a happening:
a shuffling of cards in the branches,
those parliament cries
                     reeling in tens
from the telephone lines,
as down they draw
                 into the thickening trees.
    And for time,
             calm.
A hare in the harrow field.
                  All else still.
And we turn for home, believing it done,
unequipped for the scene
            to come.

III

                                        From south,
above the Carrs,
                    they come in
                                        in their thousand.
More swarm than flock,
                        an oil smoke,
lifting the choirs from their branches –
others from outfields   as though rising through earth,
shaking the bigger soil from their backs –
until up and over the trees they funnel
                    ten
        twenty   thousand
                                more
and we crane our necks at a tumbling shoal
unsure if it's upward or down that we stare.
                                        How
we fumble for familiarity: recalling the likeness
that is not a likeness   of looking up as a child
from a bonfire, watching the ash-tufts
rise and flit and feather in the night
                                    air.
Why will the mind
make one thing like another
when some marks won't compare –
when the ghosts roost   and the cells coerce
on a scale we cannot answer;
acts no god can tidy,
                    that astound
                            and stay
long after the black birds have settled in the forest.

The Staithe

How long has it looked this way? —
these shallows glazed with sundown,
as around them, the saltings settle;
the gulls, for once, have given up on quarrel,
a woman whistles to her dog, and out
in the estuary, where the pintails nestle,
a red boat rides on a long white rope.
Further still, the curve of the earth
is unmissable; why ever did they think it flat?
In shore, butterflies bloom from the aster.
I thought there would be more time.

Deor

from the Anglo-Saxon

Weyland knew of shackles and of suffering.
Smith strong: ring-maker, sword-shaper,
master of his own, till he was slaven
to Nithhad's cold company. To keep his catch
his captor tore the tendons from his feet
and condemned a better man than he.
        These things have passed, so may this pass from me.

Baldohilda, brotherless, grieved less for them
than her own sore state – beaten, bullied, raped,
and thick with child, so that nothing in her wits
told her this would finish well.
        These things have passed, so may this pass from me.

Mathhilda's love for Geat could bring no good.
Wretched, it grew so nothing could support it;
they could not rest nor sleep for love.
        These things have passed, so may this pass from me.

For thirty years Theodric ruled the Mareing place.
His name was known to many.
        These things have passed, so may this pass from me.

Much have we heard of Emanaric's wolve
whose grip upon the Goths was rough and true,
who sent his pack among his own people.
Many endured the coarse hand of his wrath,
foresaw no peace to come, no kingdom
until his kingdom be pulled to dust.
      These things have passed, so may this pass from me.

The man who goes about his world gathering sorrow:
his mind alone moves to darkness; there seems to him
no end that he can name, no goodness there to come.
May he remember that in this world
there is a maker of change:
some are given glory, satisfaction,
others must have it taken away.

About myself I will say only this:
that once I was a poet of the Hedenings,
true to my guide, and my name was Deor.
For many years, I held this place,
and the muse was kind, until Hearonda,
the more skilful one, took the earth from under me,
the ground and the water once bestowed to me.
      These things have passed, so may this pass from me.

III

The Blackbird of Spitalfields

Four a.m. undone. No lock-ins, no vans
about their rounds, no running gangs,
just phrase on phrase of traffic heading north,
and up above the maze of roofs, a blackbird's flute,
unable to distinguish night from day.
Is it light or land that has him sing,
or fuss for unreached company? And still,
for all his thirds and major fifths,
his song not song, but simple call and speech.
Nothing sings together on this earth but us.

The Diomedes

Summers he would sail for Alaska
working the crabbers as deckhand or galley;
autumns returning with old-weather stories of
clam catchers, fur trappers, and the twin isles
of Diomede: two miles and a continent between them;
and how, in winter, when the straits froze over,
the islanders could walk from one to the other,
crossing the sheet for family, scrimshaw,
soapstone, to marry, passing the date line
that ran through the channel, stepping
between days as they went.

As far as I know he doesn't go back;
if he did, he'd hear that only the fearless
now track on foot, the pack no longer dependable
for walrus, ski-plane or the human step.

Even now, there's something to his story
I find difficult to fathom. At home, in London,
listening to my neighbours' raised voices
or catching the man opposite dressing,
I wonder what it is we will do to be neighbourly,
how part of us longs for it to matter that much,
to be willing to nudge our skin-boat into the waves,
to be between floe and another;
half-way from home, in no safety, unsure
if we're headed for tomorrow or yesterday.

Commute

Rain on the river this morning —
a reminder that some days
the world must come down:
the heron from his high bank,
the terns in lasso above Battersea
or the planes descending over Kennington.
Each will work with the weather beneath them,
taking the tutelage of tide or wind
or engine to lift themselves up.
No one can soar indefinitely.
I am giving my life to you.

4

Losing Time

Now, when clocks go back, and we take the same hour twice,
and even so it seems that something has been lost,
like a man at midday looking for his shadow,

what comes to mind is the uncalmed child –
sleepless, staring at the clock alarm – who,
asked what she is frightened of, says she is frightened of time.

This house waits for happiness. A garden two-thirds walled,
the alder and the laurel felled, an old shed
slumped about its soil: we see only our beginnings.

Night hangs between the streetlamps. A dog-fox trots
　　on an old trail.
The uncalmed child now mother of her own, sleepless
till her boy comes home, his paper hands unfastened
　　on the fold.

At Marble Hill the ash trees keep their key rings still.
The grasses thin for winter ground
and burglars dress for longer rounds.

We dug this birch bark cherry under rain, remade
the windows for the windowpanes, took April's news
from bathroom walls: we grow out of our beginnings.

The father seeks the childhood from the child.
The hour reruns.
And hounds hang on the hill.

Animal

Earth woke you at an unshook rib.
We had no books to base you on,

we had no tools to pare you down,
so incomplete,

you were both catalogue and kit,
the takings of a varied ground.

All bones became your bones.
We laid fibula to femur,

radius to humerus,
one hip crocked from female, one of male;

our ivory, uncommon kid,
from such modesty you stood.

Light wounded, wind wounded.
Water slipped from your sternum.

You pined for the forest floor,
you pined for your own kind;

but there were no kinds like yours:
so bit⁄part, out of epoch,

mocked by those from nearer shore.
We took them on and knocked them down –

damned if they cast pity on your name –
and wondered

what kind of kindness this could be,
to leave you where you could be left,

unwarranted to all but us,
circling your roof of fire and straw.

Night moves at the welter pools.
The summer slips, the winter hoars.

Eleven times the long hand crosses short;
we go so far.

One day the rings will slip from our fingers.
But not from yours. Everything

we almost are we lose. My animal,
you cannot know how hard in love you are.

The Collect

Seek rarity as old men might seek time.
By which you meant such glimpses in the grasses:

a fledgling bittern, a Norfolk Hawker,
an earthstar last seen in the war,

and now a scarce fen orchid
found on just three sites you will not name.

I've seen it, in the reed beds of the alder carr,
staked to keep it out from under foot.

You'd barely note its modesty:
its simple, yellow/greening flowers,

its humble leaves, unscented airs,
so well within the frame of ordinary.

But scarcity can lend a mind to madness,
to strain to keep in harness what must run out.

In these numb unnumbered mornings,
our tea/bags radiating in the cup,

what's common is suddenly so precious:
this sunburst through a pane of glass;

an arrow of geese
pointed somewhere south;

the toddler in the street below
who looks so far to see just up ahead,

his eyeline tilted skyward,
reaching out an ungloved hand for rain.

The Fox Runner

The winter that a fox got bold
and dragged a baby from its home,
the winter we made life all of our own:
a reynard crowned the far end of the avenue.
I'd watch it from a storey window,
king in its cuffs, hot hide pluming,
the frosted cars courtiers in jewel.

Running one night – fluorescent, scotchlite –
I found myself at sprint on it
the full length of the road.
Hard to know the more surprised.
It took my name on a notebook nose,
incredulous that I'd suppose so much.
It will define us, the dignity we choose.

Leaves

*Beam sceal on eorðan
leafum liþan, leomu gnornian.*

*A tree on earth must
lose its leaves; the branches grieve.*
— MAXIMS I, 26–7

I

Kicking up leaves in a lulled wood
when paths are covered under foot
and a low rook claps at a loose dog,
or a called name carries in the bare trees
as dry leaves flow from toe to heel;
and, slowed, the mind unfastens from its rope
like a raft admitted to a current,
draped again on a childhood boat
watching the bow⁄water splice and seal at the stern —
there and here, in one place and two.

What child was unhappy with leaves at their knees;
with red leaves tipping their boot tops, brown⁄
yellow leaves going in with their socks;
or playful with plane falls to dunk
in the hood of a duffle coat.

But the wood is not yet your childhood.
And out on a clearing, on the open slade,
three hawks hang on unseen strings.
And where the crack willows splay
like dancers spent upon their stools,

their heartwood open to audience:
the young beams of a brocket kneeling
in the grass beyond the knot, so close
his breath was felt before his bray announced him.
Four times he rose and roared, my ribcage belling,
I thought all that stood between us were those trees.

Beith. Luis. Fearn. Saille.
Call out the billywitch, call out the thunder.
Nion. Uath. Duir. Tinne.
Call out the oak⁄ox, call the horse⁄pincher.

Something has stirred in the selfsame wood.
In the woken wood. The altering wood.
Something has slipped in the semblance,
like someone in their autumn coat
who changes just their gloves each day.

What falls is not forgotten, but in time
drawn back through the bole and the branch
in the annual abscission.
All in time returned to time.
I know what time is until you ask me.

Fire will be found in the wood
and the earth fed by fire⁄ash.
And the metal forged will enrich the water
so the wood may drink before it is given to fire.

These are the phases. Five roots and four.
These are the states of change.

II

As the first snow blazed over Antrim
as London waited winter,
your mother locked in the unlit wards
of Isleworth, long beneath her landslide,
your father lost to the unmanned miles of corridor,
into this you came, furnace to flame:
deer, dear one, beloved, friend.

Frost shall freeze. Fire melt wood.
Earth grows, ice bridges, and water wears
a helmet of glass to shield its new⁄made life.
And a worn mind slips to a fire⁄pit in childhood:
wet lines looped on a cool lawn,
a wheelbarrow ferrying its deadwood and leaf⁄break –
those moss⁄run bones of broken branch
having no more and so more to give.
Cloak, smoke, barely blaze –
the flukes rose up through the copper beech leaves
as if they had somewhere to be –
out with my dad in the scarfed cold
wondering where the burnt wood went.
And ash is what cannot be taken:
potash, phosphate, calcium carbonate.
I don't even know where your ashes are.
But all that they are is in everything.
All that they are I am.
And the embers were never an ending.
But the start of our investment in the chemical earth.

III

Plugging the steel blade into the weighed soil, age one,
you lift a garden trowel for which you are too young,
bearing the load from flowerbed to flagstone
to see how it is when moved from there to here:
amazed that you can hold the earth upon a spade,
have it heap, settle and reshape, sown
with twig tips, rose leaf and petal,
your self-assembled palace from the ground.

Soon you will tell me you can touch your own shadow,
that you're angry at the sea because the waves won't listen;
you'll wonder why the moon doesn't bump into the earth,
and say you see gravity falling.
    Daddy, it's a boiling dark out there. I will
    always be here for you if you don't need me.

There will be weights you have to carry,
the kind of weight that makes the horses bow
or tradesmen tip their cap above their brow.
But every hallway will have a door
until a door's not needed any more.
Until one phase will overcome another.
And the earth drink the water that quells the fire.
And the fire melt metal that pares all wood.
And the wood pin the earth that drinks the water.
Until one commands another.

Wind is the sky's speed, but thunder is louder
in its own season. And the field will turn so fast
that it will not stir a blade of grass.

We translate to bring the outdoor in,
to be in two hands and in one:
these leaves are loaned from the endless common.
A hawk will learn a hawker's glove,
a wolf alone will languish in the wood.

When you move everything moves upon you.
When you sing you join in the chorus of everything.

The rocks will be made of the living.
And the living are made of mountains.

IV

Above the rush hour brimming on the bridge:
a foil balloon each birthday, bobbed from Kingsway
down to Waterloo – high on its helium, its *1*, then *2*,
then *3*, scrapping to be free – straining at its lead
like a greyhound after quarry – the blunt wind
barrelling off the reach, lifting clear my heels.

At Moormead fair, the string slipped through your fingers
and rose in some yet unencountered trick.
You searched at your own height, beneath the park bench
and the pram wheel; you couldn't countenance ascent:
gone to you, but going still.

Grief clings. The clouds pass on.
How best to grip the fiercety of letting go?
Everything wishes to be away,
and no one returns to tell us what heaven is like.

Time ticks. Soils shift. Your garden mound
disperses under laws too ruthless yet for us.
Neither the arrow shook from its quiver
nor the river filled from the higher stream
return as they began, nor woods reborn –
always forward, always on –
the relentless hooves and the hunting horn.

Heat dims, white pales,
hearts thin, lights fail.

Because heat is merely movement
and the cooling of metal is the cooling
of all things – in time the cooling of time –
until there is a moment without momentum,
when before is behind you and ahead
and after is behind you and ahead
and there is no longer a separation
when photons cool and these terms mean the same.

In some moments you see or think you see the join:
a kingfisher flushed from Beverley Brook –
that blue you only grasp in flight,
the painted air long out of sight;
or running from wet grass onto summer stone –
your footprints follow, heat and go;
or seeing into last year's night tonight. –
    If the sun gets too hot we'll have to blow the candles out.

That summer you spoke of things dying.
That you were, I was, all of us, dying.
Three, not even four, how could you know your meaning?
    It means that nobody is there any more.

Two are companion,
and make a third. A tree shall lose
its leaves on earth; the branches grieve.
Every traveller will reach an end.
And daily is the struggle against departure.

Light dies in the doorway. My mother's raising arm:
– Is it all right? Is it all right? I'll be wherever I am.

Earth enfolds us. The cloud-collector.
The heart's river. The life-giver.
Evening, the day's old age. The uterus.
In seven times seven days.

The wood is the spring and the fire is the summer.
And the earth is our late, long summer.
Ore brings autumn, winter bears water.
We are the watering wood.

Your house was built before you were born.
The earth was yours before you were your mother's.
But it was not prepared, and its depth was not measured
and no one has said how long it should be.
Now someone shall bring you to where you must go.
Now you shall be measured and, after you, the earth.

A red buck swam in the cold pen
and breached the bank ten yards ahead,
his hot flank steaming from the sharp lake.
He was a wonder of intimidation,
all muscle and sinew and territorial pull.
I took the ground between him and your pram
certain he would run us through;
but chill had placed a tremor in his knee:
I stepped to him, he turned at heel.

Round and round the deer and the hound
where nothing is lost but sent to ground.

A tree on earth shall lose its leaves.
But the wood that held us holds us,
and the moment we stood in is standing.
So the wood, now, is not the wood then,
advancing like a tireless queen,

its roof of new hours and axes.
And the wood, then, is not the wood now,
but a hearth of continuous elsewhere.
A heap of earth, a slipped balloon,
hot prints lifting off the warm stone,
kicking through leaves, a callable common,
in one place and in two.

Somewhere ahead of where we are we are.
Somewhere behind of where we are we also are.
I was there with you now. I am here with you then.
The park gates close to reopen.

What domineers diminishes.
What destroys will injure the destroyer.
By earth we see earth by water water.

   Maybe it would be better to be a baby
   so you didn't have to know.

A power over horses and the running of the deer.
When the doorway darkens and the waves won't listen.
And the oak knight and the holly knight duel.

   Don't leave me wherever you go.
And we won't and we won't, until.

We can never go back to the watering wood.
We go back.

A Bluebird for Rose

Ahead, in days when sight or detail darken,
I may see nothing of such single intuition
as this moment at my daughter's bedroom window:

a toy bird discovered on her bookcase
she glides, on tiptoe, against the glass,
her one-year-old's unguided grace

retracing flight,
and finding in the sky outside
a place for her belonging.

Wulf

from the Anglo-Saxon

The men of my people will hunt him as game.
They will kill him if he comes with force.

It is different with us.

Wulf is on one shore, I on another,
fast is that island, thickened with fens;
fierce are the men who guard it:
they will kill him if he comes with force.

It is different with us.

It was rainy weather, and I sat down and wept,
and grieved for my Wulf, his far wanderings,
when a battle-quick captain laid me down;
that was peace for a moment, but only a moment.

Wulf, my Wulf, it was wanting you
that made me sick, your never coming,
the unanswered heart, no mere starvation.

Do you hear, Eadwacer? Wulf will carry
our whelp to the woods.

Men easily break what is never bound.
Our song, for one.

IV

West

What is west but water.
What is west but the end of land and light.
What is there but the day rerun,
the replaying of wake and darkness.
Nothing on my line but Ladye Bay and Southerndown,
nothing but Mizen Head and ocean.
When the westerlies come I'll not be facing
the Atlantic's mind of nothing.
All I seek is a window to the east
a square of sunrise, not a shading sea.
What is west but our morning shadow,
the place you are behind me.

A Red Hairband in Iveragh

Climbing the road from Cahersiveen
we fell behind a cattle drive, a‑mile‑and‑slow
without a pass uphill –

our engine idled, your brother
summered on the bonnet, your mother, you,
gone out on foot, our cortège behind.

But nearing the farm
the collies snapped too smartly
at a yearling singled off the rear

and sent it bucking, wild
and witless, back up
the lane at you.

Scream – I

screamed for what you couldn't see:
the heifer, thirty times of you,
bearing down,

your mother's shield –
your small feet
slipping under track –

and drove at it — to ram
or force the car between —
until it slid and shook itself around.

We bailed you in the back
your plait un⁄
furled like sudden fire.

Morning on the laneway:
a scar where slots and tyres stopped
and in the few flat feet between

the shock red of your hairband
blazing as the fuchsia,
immaculate with rain.

Cara

And should you go alone to your namesake isle
to the slake, slate waters of Argyll,
the pier at Ardminish your stern,
your prow the Sound of Gigha;
should you beach within the harbour of the horses
or the black peninsula, or reach
the chapel of St Finla, the ridgeway
ramping southward out to Ulster –

go first to find the Broonie's Chair
and beg your welcome of the ùruisg,
your spirit guide, your given wish,
so clan, so like your brother's hand;
then look back to the sole house on the inch
and see the match-flare wicking in the eave,
a lamplight listening in off Moyle,
where four swans sing on a sea of oil.

Four Roads

When we're wearied under night-flare
on some recurring reel of carriageway,
may we turn from the contemporary
and overlay a tracing of the past:
the ancient lanes of Ermine and of Watling,
the unerring Fosse, and one so old
it had no need for name. To map them
is to make some version of the marvellous:
the crisscross of their founding lines,
their solar graphs and trade paths
so like the markings on a human palm,
a near-completed pentagram.
Beneath these lumens stalks of sodium,
their slipways spooling into settlement,
the roads beneath the wheels still sense the agger,
and deeper still, a single swathe through foot-worn grass:
the ceaseless pull, to grant the traveller purpose –
to begin with nothing less than our arrival.

Landlock

Rain came rarely to the white wood valley.
In between times, he did what he could,
cut rhubarb and gooseberries, brought flowers
from the hill: camel-thorn in winter, rest-harrow
in summer, rock-rose, barberry, mimosa;
he ground wormwood to temper her fever.
When the trouble was run he would take back the farm,
plant olive and cedar, build her a home.
But she thought mostly of sea —

                            the uncommissioned sea —

wild at her, salt strong — not the starving river,
brackish and torn — a river is never enough.
One of her wishes was to find her own way,
but the lowlands were locked down, the plains undone;
so they climbed and climbed as one.
And when she could not walk he carried her
and when he could not carry her she walked.
Such as this the days went by, till his strength was wrung.
He laid his back against the longer rock
and set her head that gently in his lap.
Sleep overcame them on the slope.
He woke to take the sunlight in his eyes
and could not see at first the greater distance,
the strained blue stain blue light in the distance,
that seemed each part to move — how could it? —

a thin drawn band of sea, somewhere meeting sky.
He raised her head that she might see it done.
But where she was she had already gone.

The Mansion

There were two lives locked in an unlocked room.
One opened the left door, the other the right. They went on.

In the next room the doors were left and right.
Each was alone while the other was near. They went on.

Though the doors they had passed through were only two,
there were three rooms between them and two more doors.

If one took only the right, the other the left,
would they converge? But deeper into the house they went.

There were two locked lives in an unlocked room.
One returned while the other advanced.

But the unlocked room was not the same room
in a house no longer their own.

Hedge Bird

You're almost home. You've been numb
a long time. You didn't see the daylight slip out,
nor the fieldfares raiding the windfalls;
you didn't notice the holly in fruit,
or the wind lift daphne and whin
to your nose. Dusk gloves the hill;
soon the woods will back into shadow.
You could lose your way, even still.

Something is calling from the thicket.
You know the song, it was with you
when you started. Try not to think
you can find it with your eyes, reach out
and you'll only silence it. Listen.
The world comes in by the ear,
nudging the spirit to here and there,
waking the heart⁄step, conjuring the air.

Turn into the lane, the house is in view.
She loves you. You will make it through.

Havener

I

Near burr far rain. No water cart on Heigham Sound,
no old moon carried in a new moon's lap.
A white owl loops at Piccamore Loke,
a pipistrelle on Candle Dyke. The cutters say
that when the reed-top feathers close the downpour comes;
that one thing answers from another:
you, from a south-west peninsula,
this, your place of found water.
Here I took your lesson in self-learning,
worked the low arch on the Thurne, the tidal arm
at Breydon; and when your dad slipped Womack bank
how I fetched him up you said was like a merman
and that you knew I would, as trust was what
you traded in, and what we earned a clearance.

We're long below the Hundred Stream,
our dayboat whirring back to Stalham.
How deep my daughter sleeps within your arms,
how tight you hold her even as you doze.
A yary sun, the Koniks' caper, a king-
fisher writing light across the bow;
and upriver, at Mud Half-mile, a bittern
in the reach of Irstead Shoals, its wingbeat bowed,
its shoulder slung, a weight too large for sky to hold,
so low I might have plucked it down.
But you are sleeping now and not to be disturbed.

Astern, the turbulence through which we'd passed.
Ahead, new water still as glass. All you love
all you loved reflecting back on you

•

Hant, tant, tuthery, furthery, fant.
When leaf is off the reed is cut.
Sarny, darny, downy, dominy, dick.
After that the colts come.

•

Hoving out from Halvergate on some kind of fen music:
a typewriter train and its ribbon of carriages
boxes of matchmen crossing the marshes.
Nearer in, the black sail of the Albion.
The marshmen say a wherry's not properly laden
till a robin can drink from her decks –
down to her bins, full lading – a loom
so large the air around her darkens, till she spills
her wind on the weather-bank and ghosts.

It was believed that the best of boats
could move by themselves – Atet or Argo
or Skíðblaðnir – crossing between wind
and water to sail a sky-realm –
for Hy-Brasil or the Fortunate Isles
or to capture the light of the sun,
then to fold like cloth in a pocket
having known the ocean as firmament:
boundless, open to the infinite.

II

We found a closeness keeping in the fire
and made it up: an undercourse of newspaper,
wood split in the stable yard, two vents
of polished brass, sinking the scuttle
into its shallow of coal. Sundays
in the window bays with football tables and the news,
beneath the mantelpiece you boughtfrom salvage:
its apron carving of the Lucerne Lion,
all mane and muscle, dying on its shield.
Still now I can't discern the subtlety of symbol:
a force abroad, a guard without a people,
caught between civilities and change;
the spear run deep, the shield warmed.
Too much has happened here to make it home.

•

So comes a summer of fire and smoke
now that ash is out before the oak
when March buys winter's coat
and sells it three days afterward.

•

Your father rode his mule to school
and slept on warm days in the wood
and laid tar on the old man's gate
and sold his catch to pay the debts
and worked your whooping cough at night
and unionised for those in tied
and watched your school bus strain between
the hills, on which, until the last,
you said you didn't do enough
to save the Roma kids from taunt.
We never knew you shirk a fight
for those unharboured or unheard:
rights, a living wage, hot water.
In this city now they call you daughter.

III

It isn't easy to observe, far less define,
but coming home alone you sense the company of others
who knew the need to build was more than building,
more than merely lime and clay and sand;
that strength lay deeper than the course of brickwork,
deeper than the bond; that halls could be a heartway
blooming into undrawn rooms, kitchens
leading hearthward finding light.
Someone saw it before it could be seen
and set the vision waking, no longer dreamt
but dream: doorways onto sunbreak, a brace
of keys, a garden glimpsed by day.
Somewhere for our lives to try.
A roof to raise us closer to the sky.

•

I have made a hole in my manners.
I have laid a stone at your door.
The dog that fetches will carry.
Your tired eyes draw straws.

•

She'd called their talk earthy,
those children in the lane to school
on cobweb mornings such as these
when corn was bent and baffled in the wind.
We'd hear them talk of 'futnon', meaning
now and then, every foot anon. Their
fathers took a pheasant *futnon*, a hare,
and so on. And on the rond, on winter
wartime mornings, their father's fathers
heard the sirens calling out at sea,
and *futnon* heard the bitterns answering;
and one, who let his hands fall to his side
to find he'd clasped a mother's upturned beak,
unprepared for any cost to leave her nest behind.

IV

I think now of the kite
you gave the children

being not from you
but you

the lift that takes us into air
how the weight upholds us

that thrust and drag
all dip and dance at the bridle

and far below your grandchild
finds the limit of the spool

her body arched and straining
a wild line into light

wrangling for sky‑horse
or some impossible catch

trying for all she has
to pull you back to earth.

•

Wheat lies best in wet sheets.
If you swear you will catch no fish.
A fathom of shooves, a shoof of hands.
To sit where the dog was hanged.

•

First out, last home: the clock-watch of rooks,
till airs come on and they're in before noon

when the wind brings in as the storm-cock sings
and the rain-bird laughs in the grass.

Out in the channel there's a large sea running
and a backing blow that will bring no good

that a crow sees coming but a crab does not
and clings on stubborn to a crabbing pot.

Seagull, seagull, sit on the sand
it's never good weather when you're on land

when the daws roost low and the sundogs rise
and the pigs run about with the straw

when spiders won't spin but become their own guttering
and the rope comes hard to untwist

and cattle heap up in the midfield
as horses gain cover. Far burr near rain.

•

And then it comes your western rain,
your wind⁄west, rain's⁄nest Mewstone rain,

this rain⁄off⁄known⁄water, opening east:
a fox's wedding, then a hammering like hoof⁄fall

as one thing succumbs another. And now
when I hear downpour I think of Aonbharr,

wind⁄speed, taking as one the land and sea;
or Arvak and Alsvinn, harnessing sun,

a wolf at their heels who'll one day catch them.
Until then the chase is magnificent:

sea⁄foam and fire⁄hooves where the sky⁄boat goes
and Wave⁄Sweeper tilts in the shallow.

Daily gets easier to loosen the rope.
Plenty of ladybirds, plenty of hope.

The child unmoors in its mother's hands.
The trees talk of rain long after the rain disbands.

Headland

Coast in its cave like a walled bear,
Not caring to be quartered or subdued,
Though it bides for a floodtide or slips
Into strata or reforms into air
It cannot die, being there at the dawn,
Being half of me. If only I could climb down
From the headland, down between the needle
And the shore, I might again make time.
But dusk comes, and I have places of my own,
And I did not think to stay long, just longer,
With those who share in whatever may be:
The half in us that ages, the half that finds eternity.

Ruin

from the Anglo-Saxon

Rare is this wrought-work, downed by design;
civilities collapse: even giants must die.
The roofs unroofed, the towers in dust,
their beams unburdened and frost-locked.
All that was raised has fallen, all in time
undermined. Grasped in the ground
in the harsh, gripped ground:
the makers and masons, their centuries' kin.
Time and again, bone grey and blooded,
this wall saw storms and stood; no more.

HERE THERE WAS FIRE

The mind knew what must be done –
bind the ties, secure the rings, a foundation of chains –
it knew wonders: such space to move in,
such waters to draw, such far-sight and vantage
that voices would sing, having known their own tale
to sing about. And then came the change.
And the wrecking was absolute. The end of days.
An end takes even the brave. Defence
gave way to wasteland, strongholds knelt
in the rubble. Those who might have repaired
were nowhere to be found. And now these halls
lie empty, no shade afforded by the bared roofs,
where company once had cause,

something in which to believe:
plans of purpose, the splendour of tomorrow,
vine⁄ripe, and war⁄shined;
so much of value to look upon, so
precious, the sheer stones of the earth
and all that came from them:
an unshakeable house, a hot spring,
a garden walled on three sides,
some place to bathe, to heat
the heart. That was a moment.

AND HERE ALSO THERE WAS FIRE

PLACE NOTES

§

I

CAUSEWAY: Lindisfarne, Northumberland, 11 April 2012.

THE SEA STICK: St Bees Head, Cumbria, July 2005.

BECK: Pelter Bridge, Under Loughrigg, River Rothay, Cumbria, 13 October 2005.

WASTWATER: Hardknott Pass, Wasdale, Cumbria, 4 October 2005.

THE WHITE HART OF SYKESIDE: High Sykeside, Grasmere Town End, Cumbria, 27 February 2006.

ALL THERE EVER IS: Great Rigg, Grasmere Vale, 25 February 2006.

CALL: Alcock Tarn, Grasmere Vale, 7 August 2005.

STONES: Greenhead Gill, Grasmere Vale, 15 May 2006.

THE LONG SNOW: Easedale Tarn, Easedale, Cumbria, 19 March 2006.

LONE: Exeter Book (115r–v), 7 September 2007: C8th Northumbrian or Mercian Anglian dialect likely, West Saxon later; MS untitled, commonly 'The Wife's Lament', first as 'Exile's Complaint' (1826).

II

ANGLIA: River Stour, Manningtree, Essex–Suffolk border, 7 February 2009.

IKEN: St Botolph, Iken, Suffolk, 13 March 2015.

A HARNSER FOR JAMES: Blakeney Harbour, Norfolk, 16 August 2011: *barley-bird*, nightingale; *bishybarnabee*, ladybird; *develin*, swift; *dodman*, snail (Norf.); *erriwiggle*, earwig; *hay-jack*, whitethroat; *haysele*, season of making hay; *hin*, chicken; *hodmedod*, snail (Suff.); *hoss*, horse; *jacob*, frog; *jasper*, wasp; *merrymay*, mayfly; *minifer*, stoat or weasel, specifically ermine; *pishamire*, ant; *pollywiggle*, tadpole; *ranny*, shrew.

WINTERTON NESS: Winterton-on-Sea, Norfolk, 26 December 2010.

I WILL LIFT UP MY EYES: Scolt Head Island, Norfolk, 26 August 2017: *Levavi oculous*, Marion Campbell.

WHERE NARROW WATER WIDENS: Breydon Water, Norfolk, 29 November 2016.

THE ISLAND: Scolt Head Island, Norfolk, 24 July 2015.

ROOKS: Buckenham Carrs, Norfolk, 15 February 2011: At dusk, sometime between 5–6, fifty or sixty rooks overhead, east, to a coppice of trees that I could not make out in the half-dark. They made such a noise that I did not hear those approaching in a second, larger flock, looked up by chance at hundreds overhead; perhaps what the blitz might have looked like. As they approached those in the trees they began to call and bank and veer: it seemed to me that I was watching a shoal of fish or the ashed embers of a bonfire rising into the night sky. Those too settled on the dark trees, and for twenty minutes, calm. But then from the west and from south across the marshes others came, in their many thousands. I'd never seen so many birds or heard such chorus – quite untroubled by the high winds and cold rain. The first flocks lifted from the black coppice and the vast, twisting ball of animals circles the Carrs for ten minutes before going in. It was utterly mysterious, utterly breath-taking. (Notebook)

THE STAITHE: Brancaster Staithe, Norfolk, 26 February 2011.

DEOR: Exeter Book (100r–100v), 19 May 2006: mixed dialect, likely W. Saxon copy of C5–10th Anglian origin; MS untitled, commonly as here, first as 'Scaldic Poem' (1826).

III

THE BLACKBIRD OF SPITALFIELDS: Spitalfields, London, 13 January 2009.

THE DIOMEDES: Spitalfields, London, 7 January 2007.

COMMUTE: Thames Riverboat, Putney Bridge–Blackfriars Bridge, London, 15 July 2010.

LOSING TIME: Marble Hill, St Margarets, London, 2 January 2013.

ANIMAL: Sedgwick Museum, Cambridge, 18 March 2013.

THE COLLECT: undisclosed, Norfolk Broads, & St Margarets, London, 26 January 2016.

THE FOX RUNNER: St Margarets, London, 15 February 2013.

LEAVES: Richmond Park, London, 30 September 2012:   I *Beith*, birch; *Luis*, rowan; *Fearn*, alder; *Saille*, willow; *Nion*, ash; *Uath*, hawthorn; *Duir*, oak; *Tinne*, holly: Ogham tree alphabet;   *billywitch, thunder, oak-ox, horse-pincher*: English folk-names for the stag beetle; *I know what time is*, St Augustus of Hippo, *Confessions*, XI, 14;   *Fire will be found*, Sheng, the generating cycle.

II *Frost shall freeze*, Maxims, I–B, 71–4, Exeter Book (88v–92r).

III *every hallway*, Maxims, II, 36, Cotton Tiberius B i (115r–v); *Until one phase*, Ke, the controlling cycle; *Wind is the sky's speed*, Maxims, II, 3–4; *A hawk*, Maxims, II, 17–19.

IV *Grief clings*, Maxims, II, 13; *no one returns*, Maxims, II, 63–6; *Heat dims*, Latin–English Proverbs, 3–4, Cotton Faustina A x (100v); *Two are companion*, Maxims, I–A, 23–9; *Earth enfolds us*, Empedocles, *Fragments*, 148–153a.

V *The wood is the spring*, Wu Xing, the five phases; *Your house was built*, 'The Grave', 1–6, MS Bodley 343 (170r); *What domineers*, Cheng, the overacting cycle; *What destroys*, Wu, the weakening cycle; *By earth we see earth*, Empedocles, *Fragments*, 109.

A BLUEBIRD FOR ROSE: St Margarets, London, 15 February 2015.

WULF: Exeter Book (100v–101r), 17 November 2006: C9th, written down C10, W. Saxon dialect; MS untitled, commonly 'Wulf and Eadwacer', first as 'Riddle I' (1842).

IV

WEST: Marble Hill, London–Mizen Head, Co. Cork, 7 January 2016.

A RED HAIRBAND IN IVERAGH: Dreenagree, Sneem, Co. Kerry, 9 August 2019.

CARA: Cara Island, Argyll and Bute, 13 April 2018.

FOUR ROADS: Fosse Way, Watling Street, Ermine Street, Icknield Way, 31 August 2015.

LANDLOCK: unspecified, 17 July 2009.

THE MANSION: unspecified, 18 September 2015.

HEDGE BIRD: unspecified, 9 November 2007.

HAVENER: Hickling Broad, Norfolk, & Wembury Peninsula, Devon, 19 February 2020: I *burr*, a moon halo; a *water cart* in the sky indicates rain; if a *new moon* 'carries the old moon in her lap' then storms are coming; *yary*, a morning sun, particularly yellow in colour; *Hant, tant*, shepherd's counting system; *down to her bins*, low in the water; *full lading*, a full load; *weather-bank*, wind side (Norf.).

II *ash before oak*, in for a soak *also* fire and smoke; *March buys winter's coat*, seasonal change (E. Anglian).

III *made a hole*, disgrace oneself; *laid a stone*, a symbolic token, not to call again; *dog that fetches*, a talebearer tells tales of, as well as to, you; *draw straws*, tired or sleepy; *rond*, swampy margin of a river, broad or marsh (Norf.).

IV *Wheat lies best*, thrives after a wet winter; *fathom of shooves*, in the reed-cutters' counting system six shooves make a fathom, seven half-hands make a shoof; *where the dog was hanged*, a succession of mishaps; *rooks*, will stop feeding and go home by midday in bad weather; *storm-cock*, a mistle thrush male, one of the few birds to sing as thunderstorms approach; *rain-bird*, a green woodpecker, sounds a 'laughing' call when rain is on the way; *sea running*, a large swell comes in before a wind, a warning for fishermen; *backing blow*, a rising, counterclockwise wind; *crows, crabs*, crows and gulls see the bad weather coming, but a crab will hang on to the top of a net or pot rather than seek shelter; *Seagull, seagull*, common observation usually concluding 'on land', though Norf. has been heard to repeat 'sand'; *daws*, jackdaws and crows will roost in lower branches during high wind; *sundog*, a halo either side of the sun indicating wind and rain; *pigs*, were said to be able to see wind, and would take straw into their mouths before a storm; *spiders*, hang beneath their webs in rain with legs pointing down to act as guttering; *rope*, common observation; *cattle* huddle or 'heap up' together in the fields and face into bad weather, whereas *horses* will make for the sheltered end of a field long before its arrival (Norf.); *wind-west*, 'Wind west, / Rain's nest.', common saying; *fox's wedding*, a sunshower, rain falling from a clear sky (Devonshire).

HEADLAND: unspecified, 13 October 2015.

RUIN: Exeter Book (123v–124v), 7 September 2017: early C8th, probable W. Mercian Anglian, later W. Saxon, likely setting of Bath; MS untitled, commonly 'The Ruin', first as 'The Ruined Wall-stone' (1826), missing portions where damaged by burning wood or charcoal fragment.

§

Acknowledgements are due to the following publications and broad-casts: *Analog Sea Review*, *Arts Daily Podcast* (Classic FM), *The Dark Horse*, *Earth Shattering: Ecopoems* (Bloodaxe Books, 2007), *The Echo Chamber* (BBC Radio 4), *Empty Nest: Poems for Families* (Picador, 2021), *Guardian*, *Hwaet! Twenty Years of Ledbury Poetry Festival* (Bloodaxe Books, 2016), *Identity Parade: New British and Irish Poets* (Bloodaxe Books, 2010), *Land of Three Rivers: The Poetry of North-East England* (Bloodaxe Books, 2017), *Literary Review*, *London Review of Books*, *Lung Jazz: Young British Poets for Oxfam* (Cinnamon Press, 2012), *Magma Poetry*, *The Map and the Clock: A Laureate's Choice of the Poetry of Britain and Ireland* (Faber & Faber, 2016), *Modern Poetry in Translation*, *New Statesman*, *Oxford Magazine*, *Oxford Poetry*, *PEN International*, *Ploughshares*, *Poetry Review*, *The Reader Magazine*, *The Rialto*, *Thresholds: Ten Poems by Ten Poets at Ten University of Cambridge Museums and Collections* (University of Cambridge Museums, 2013), *Trees in the City: Poems About the Need for Action on Climate Change* (Axon, 2007), *Waterlog: Journeys Around an Exhibition* (Film & Video Umbrella, 2007), *The Word Exchange: Anglo-Saxon Poems in Translation* (W. W. Norton, 2011), *Write Where We Are Now* (Manchester University).

For commissions, residencies and assistance I am grateful to the following organisations: Aldeburgh Music, Arts Council England, Bristol Festival of Ideas, British Council, Broadland Housing, Literature Across Frontiers, Norfolk Wherry Trust, Poet in the City, Poetry Archive, Sedgwick Museum of Earth Sciences, Society of Authors, Wordsworth Trust, Writers' Chain; and to the following individuals: Margaret Dye, Helen Taylor, Siân Williams and Robert Woof.

For literary advice, my thanks are due to Sarah Chalfant at the Wylie Agency, to Jessica Bullock and Alba Ziegler-Bailey.

For their expertise in design, thank you to Eleanor Crow and to Jonathan Gibbs, and, in typography, to Kate Ward.

For textual advice in their editions I am deeply indebted to Daphne Astor at Hazel Press for *Leaves*, Hans van Eijk at Bonnefant Press for *Havener*, Andrew McNeillie at Clutag Press for *East*, and Graham Moss at Incline Press for *Stones*.

These poems have benefitted from the scrupulous criticism of Carol Ann Duffy, Antony Dunn, Hamish Ironside, Bernard O'Donoghue, Clare Pollard, Jacob Polley, Neil Rollinson and Jean Sprackland, and of Lavinia Singer, who looked beyond; and from the encouragement of Neil Belton, Julia Blackburn, Ronald Blythe, Tim Dee, John Haffenden and Claire Sands.

Neil Astley was a meticulous editor and ring-maker through all seasons: *Til sceal on eðle domes wyrcean*; Pamela Robertson-Pearce brought flowers in winter.

Loving thanks to them all, and to my family.

In memory of Mum.

§